THE NATURE KIDS GUIDE TO
BALD EAGLES

DAVID ANDERSON

LP Media Inc. Publishing
Text copyright © 2026 by LP Media Inc.
All rights reserved.

For information address LP Media Inc. Publishing,
30012 Variolite St NW, Princeton MN 55371
www.lpmedia.org

Publication Data

Bald Eagles
The Nature Kid's Guide to Bald Eagles — First edition.

Summary: "Learn all about Bald Eagles, the Nature Kid Way"
— Provided by publisher.

ISBN: 979-8-89818-145-1

[1. Bald Eagles – Non-Fiction] I. Title.

Title: The Nature Kid's Guide to Bald Eagles

CONTENTS

WATERSIDE WONDERS

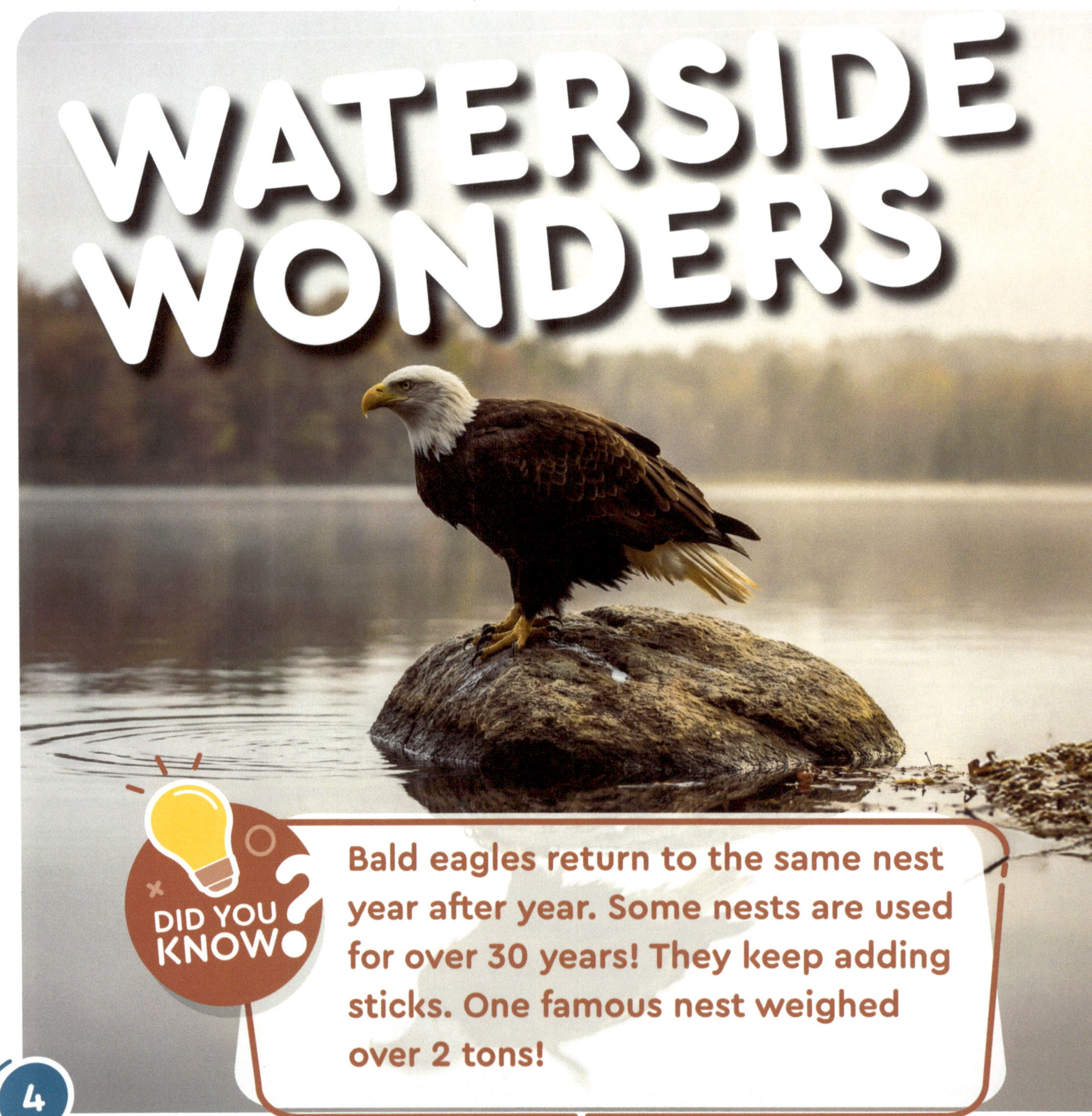

Bald eagles return to the same nest year after year. Some nests are used for over 30 years! They keep adding sticks. One famous nest weighed over 2 tons!

Screech! A bald eagle lands on a rock. It folds its wings and looks around.

Bald eagles live near water. They need lakes, rivers, and coasts to survive. Water gives them food and a place to hunt.

These birds build homes in tall trees. They pick trees close to the water's edge. This helps them spot fish swimming below.

Bald eagles like quiet places. They stay away from busy cities. Forests, wetlands, and ocean shores all make perfect homes.

Clean water is important for bald eagles. Healthy rivers mean healthy eagles!

EAGLES EVERYWHERE

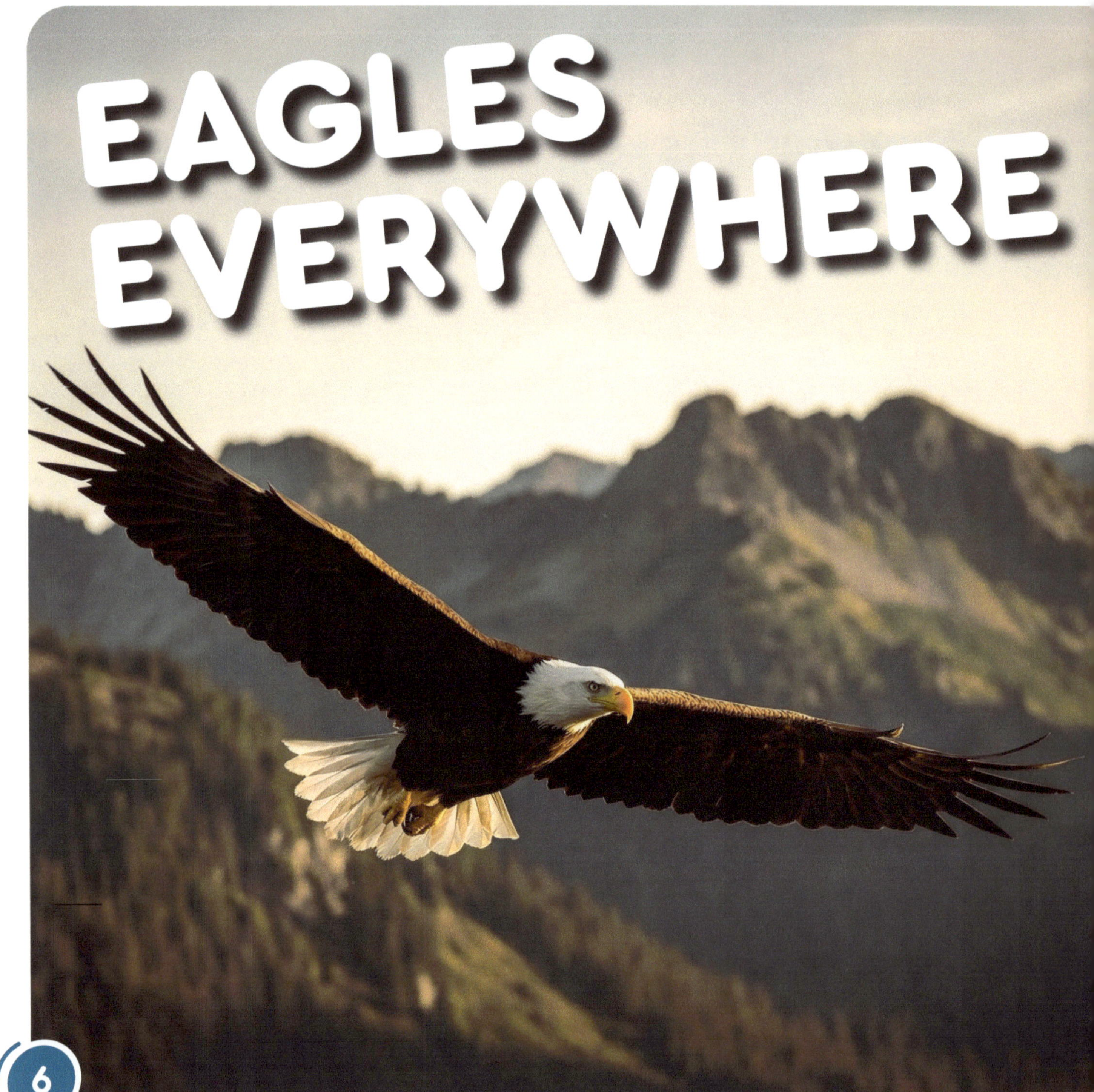

Swoosh! A bald eagle soars over a mountain. It flies far across the sky.

Bald eagles live in North America. You can find them in all 50 states! Alaska has the most. About 30,000 pairs live there.

These birds travel far. Some fly over 2,000 miles each year. They follow rivers and coastlines, searching for fish and warmer weather during winter.

Bald eagles also live in Canada and Mexico. They make homes in many different places.

Bald eagles can spot a rabbit from 2 miles away. Their eyes are 4 times sharper than ours!

BIG BIRDS

Whoosh! A bald eagle spreads its wings wide on a branch.

Bald eagles can fly up to 30 miles per hour. They can also dive up to 100 miles per hour! These big birds are super fast.

Bald eagles can weigh up to 14 pounds. Females are larger than males. That makes them one of the biggest birds in North America.

Their huge wings are what help them fly so fast. A bald eagle's **wingspan** can reach 8 feet across!

A bald eagle's body is about 3 feet long. That is as long as a yardstick!

BUILT TOUGH

Snap! A bald eagle opens it's sharp yellow beak.

Bald eagles have strong bodies. Their bones are hollow but very tough. This makes them light enough to fly but strong enough to hunt.

Their beaks are made of **keratin**. That is the same stuff in your fingernails! A bald eagle's beak is sharp and curved to tear fish apart.

Eagle feet are powerful too. Each foot has four toes with sharp **talons**. These curved claws can grip with about 400 pounds of pressure!

Bald eagle feathers are waterproof! A special oil gland helps them stay dry.

EAGLE EYES

Click! A bald eagle turns its head. Its eyes lock on a fish below.

Bald eagles have amazing eyesight. They can spot prey from miles away! Their eyes are almost as big as human eyes.

Eagles see more colors than people do. They can even see ultraviolet light.

Each eye can focus on different things at once. This helps them hunt from high in the sky.

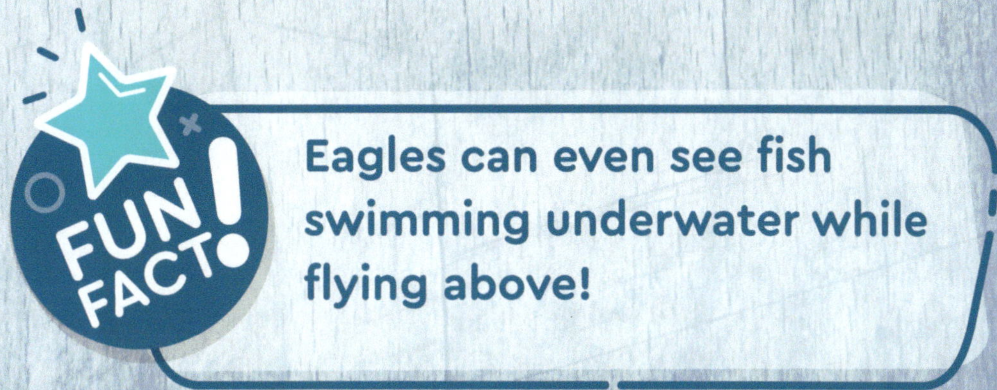

STAY SAFE

Puff! A bald eagle puffs up its feathers. It looks big and scary.

Bald eagles have ways to stay safe. Their large size keeps scares off many animals. Most predators do not want to fight such a big bird.

Eagles use their sharp talons to defend themselves. They can scratch and grab attackers. Their hooked beaks are powerful weapons too.

When in trouble, bald eagles make high-pitched whistling sounds. These calls warn other eagles of danger.

Bald eagles can flip upside down and lock talons with attackers in midair!

15

FISH FEAST

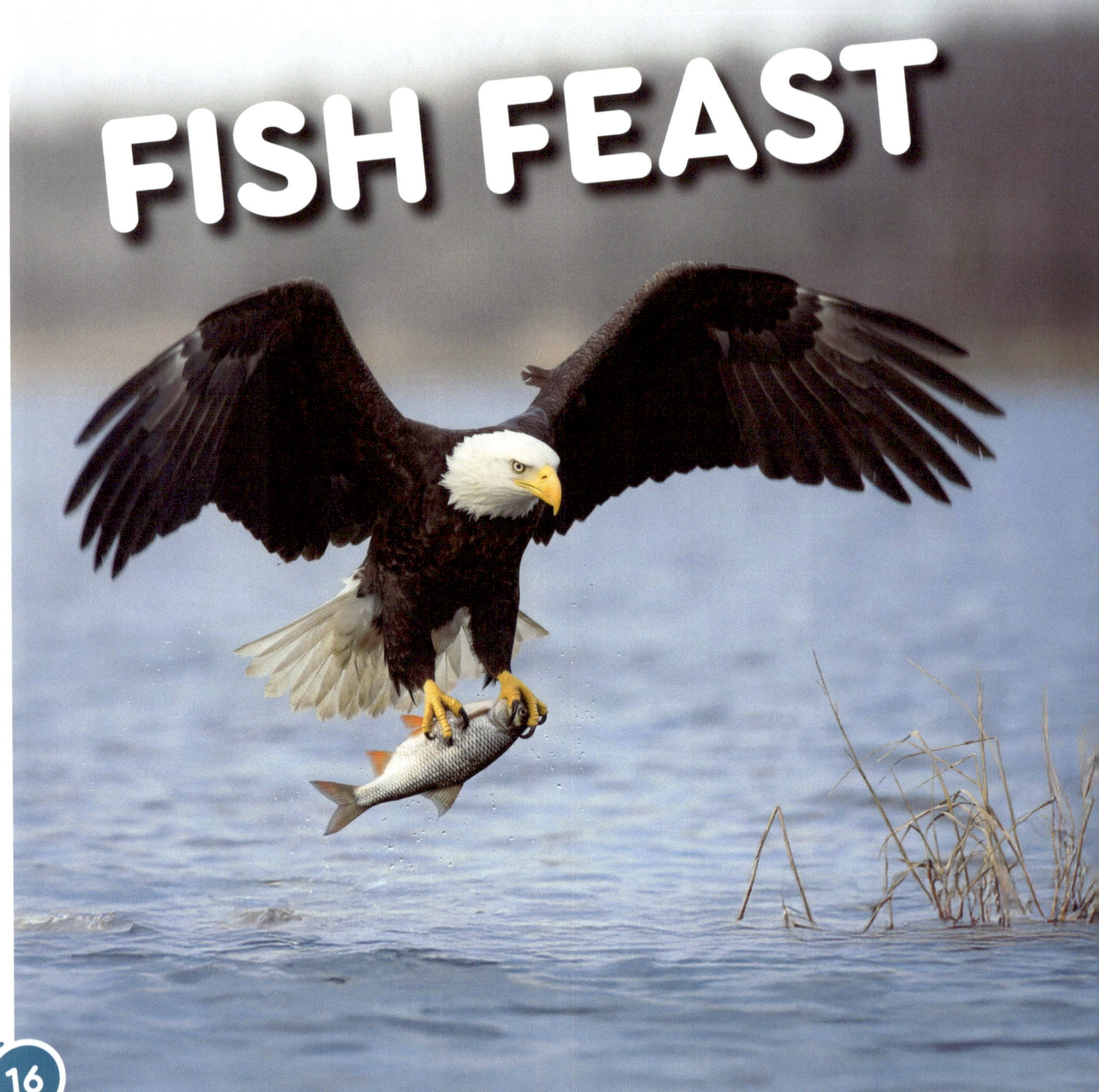

Splash! A bald eagle grabs a fish from the water. Dinner is served!

Bald eagles like to eat fish. Fish make up most of their diet, so they hunt near lakes, rivers, and coasts.

But bald eagles will eat other animals too. They catch ducks, rabbits, and small mammals. Sometimes they even steal food from other birds!

Bald eagles eat dead animals too. This helps clean up nature. In winter, they often find deer that did not survive the cold.

Eagles can store two pounds of food in their crop!

17

DIVE DOWN

Swoosh! A bald eagle dives fast, swooping low over the water.

Bald eagles are skilled hunters. They soar high in the sky and watch the water below. When they see a fish, they dive down fast.

Eagles can reach speeds of 100 miles per hour when diving! As they drop, they stretch out their legs and open their **talons** wide.

At the last moment, eagles swing their feet forward. Their rough toes help them grip slippery fish tightly. This lets eagles catch fish up to 4 pounds without landing in the water.

Bald eagles get most of their water from the fish they eat! They rarely have to drink anything.

WATCH OUT

A raccoon climbs toward a nest. An eagle watches.

Bald eagles face few predators as adults. Their size and strength keep most animals away. But eggs and young eaglets are in danger.

Raccoons climb trees to steal eggs from nests. Great horned owls, crows, and other eagles hunt eaglets. Crows sometimes attack nests in groups.

Adult eagles guard their nests closely. They chase away any animal that comes too near. But bears sometimes raid nests anyway!

FLY FAST

Squawk! A bald eagle flaps hard and fast. It escapes!

Bald eagles stay safe by being big, fast, and staying up high. Adults are so large that very few animals try to attack them

Height is an eagle's best protection. Eagles choose the tallest trees for resting. Sitting up high, they can spot danger long before it arrives. Their incredible eyesight helps them see enemies from far away, giving them plenty of time to escape.

SOARING HIGH

Whoooosh! A bald eagle glides without flapping once.

Bald eagles are amazing fliers. They use warm air currents called **thermals**. These rising pockets of air lift eagles higher and higher.

Eagles spread their wings wide to catch thermals. They can soar for hours without flapping. This saves energy!

Their long 8 foot wingspan help them glide.

Bald eagles can fly at heights over 10,000 feet! That is almost two miles above the ground.

DAILY LIFE

Chirp! The sun rises. A bald eagle wakes in its nest.

Bald eagles start their day early. They wake up at dawn. The morning light helps them see fish in the water.

Eagles spend hours perched in trees. They watch the water below. When they spot food, they fly down to grab it.

After eating, eagles rest and preen their feathers. They use their beaks to clean each feather. This keeps them ready to fly.

Bald eagles can spend up to 98 percent of their day just perching and watching for food!

27

LONER LIFE

Rustle! A bald eagle sits on a branch. No other eagles are near.

Bald eagles like to be alone. They like to hunt by themselves. Only in spring they will come together to find a mate and raise babies.

A pair of eagles may claim a territory of 1 to 2 square miles! They chase away other eagles that come too close.

But in winter, bald eagles gather in big groups. Hundreds may crowd around rivers and lakes where fish are easy to catch.

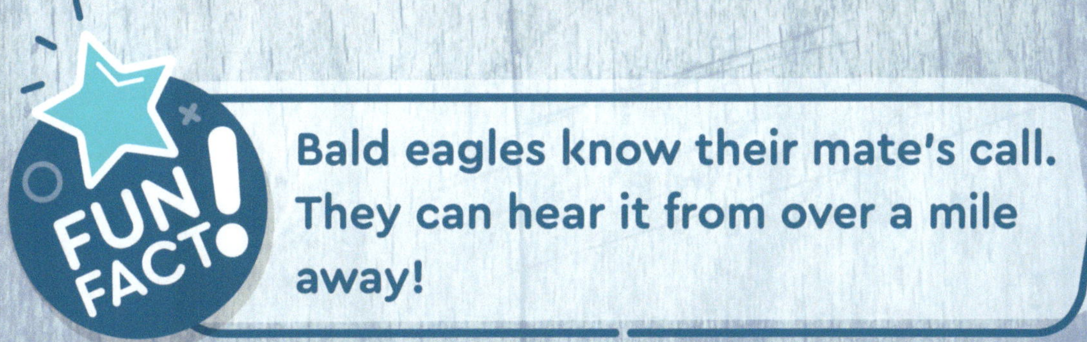

Bald eagles know their mate's call. They can hear it from over a mile away!

SKY DANCE

Two bald eagles lock claws. They spin down toward the earth.

Bald eagles do a special sky dance. Two eagles fly up high. They lock their claws together. Then they spin toward the ground.

This spin is called a cartwheel display. The eagles let go just before they hit the ground. Then they fly back up.

This daring dance is part of eagle courtship. The spinning birds can drop hundreds of feet before letting go!

Eagles can spin toward the ground at amazing speeds before breaking apart just in time!

FLUFFY EAGLETS

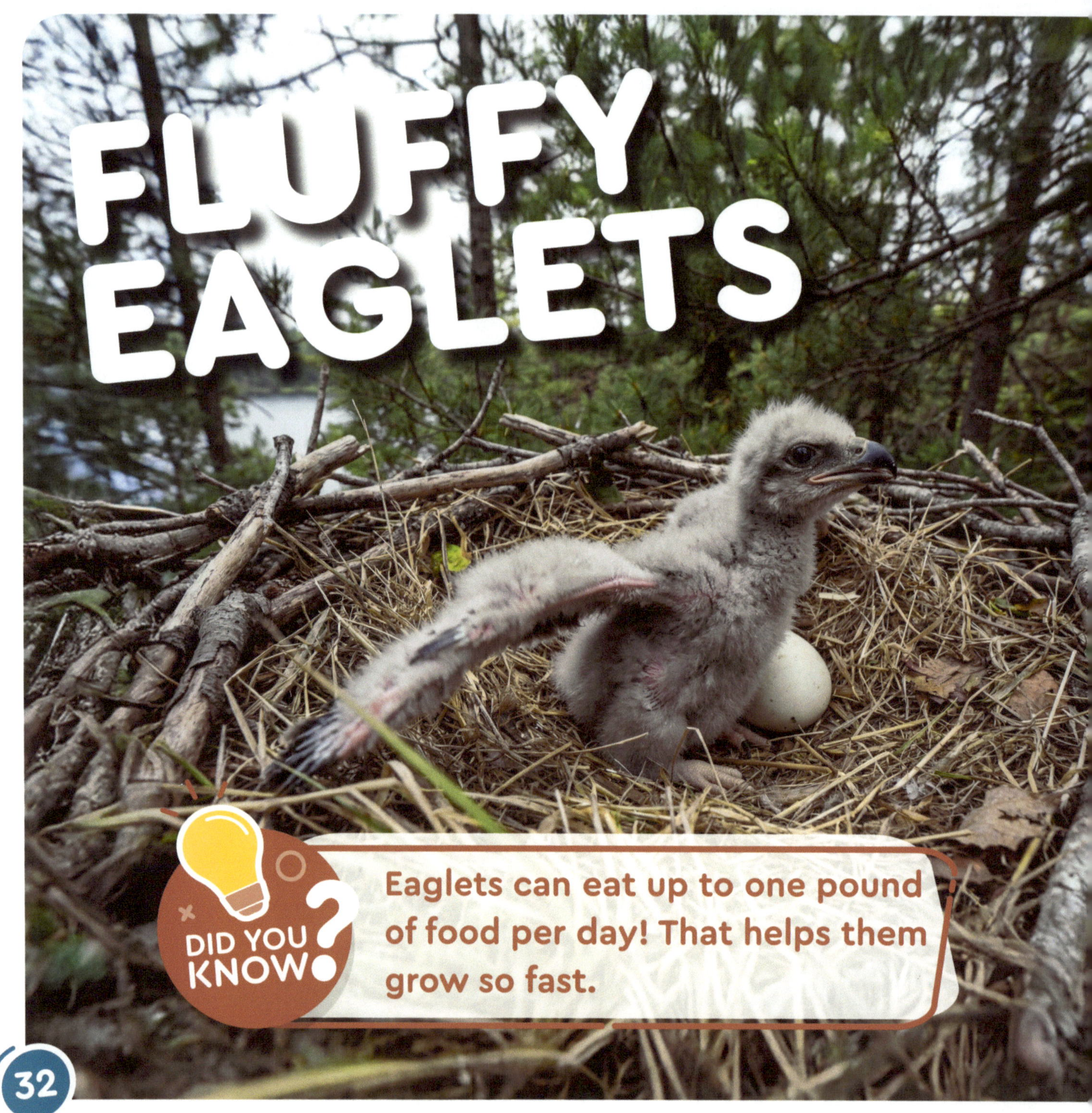

Peep! A fuzzy gray eaglet stretches in its big nest.

Baby bald eagles are called eaglets. They hatch from eggs after about 35 days. Newborn eaglets weigh only 3 ounces.

Eaglets have soft gray down feathers. These fluffy feathers keep them warm, but eaglets cannot fly yet. Their parents bring food to the nest.

Eaglets grow fast. They can gain six ounces every day. By 10 weeks old, they are almost as big as their parents. Young eagles leave the nest at about 12 weeks.

PROUD
PARENTS

A parent eagle guards its nest. It won't leave until babies are safe.

Bald eagle parents work hard to raise their young. Both the mother and father take turns sitting on the eggs to keep them warm.

Once the eggs hatch, parents bring food to the nest many times each day. They tear meat into tiny pieces for small eaglets. As eaglets grow, parents bring bigger pieces.

Bald eagle parents also protect their nest fiercely. If any animal comes too close, they chase it away.

Both eagle parents have a brood patch that gets extra warm to heat eggs!

BOUNCE BACK

A bald eagle perches tall. This proud bird almost vanished. Now it thrives!

Bald eagles almost vanished from America. In the 1960s, only about 400 pairs were left.

Pollution in rivers and lakes made eagles sick. Hunters also shot too many of them. Baby eagles had trouble surviving.

People made new laws to protect eagles and keep their homes safe. Now over 300,000 bald eagles live in North America!

Bald eagles left the endangered list in 2007. There are now over 71,000 pairs in the US!

SPOT ONE

A bald eagle sits on a tall tree. Can you spot it?

You might be able to see a bald eagle near you! The best place to look is near water: lakes, rivers, and coasts where eagles hunt for fish.

Scan the tops of tall trees for large dark birds. Adults are easy to spot with their bright white heads. Young eagles are brown with white patches.

Try looking early in the morning. Eagles often rest in dead trees with open views.

FUN FACT!

Bald eagles can turn their heads almost 270 degrees since they cannot move their eyes!

GLOSSARY

talons
Sharp, curved claws on a bird's feet used for grabbing things.

keratin
The hard material that makes up your fingernails and eagle beaks.

thermals
Warm bubbles of air that rise up and help birds float in the sky.

wingspan
How wide a bird's wings are when stretched all the way out.

crop
A pouch in a bird's throat where food is stored before it moves to the stomach.